101 SECRETS FROM A POKÉMON MASTER

101 SECRETS FROM A POKÉMON MASTER

An Unofficial Guide for

PokéMon GO players

JUSTIN RYAN

Sky Pony Press
New York

Sky Pony Press books may be purchased in bulk at special discounts for sales
promotion, corporate gifts, fund-raising, or educational purposes. Special
editions can also be created to specifications. For details, contact the Special
Sales Department, Sky Pony Press, 307 West 36th Street, 11th Floor,
New York, NY 10018 or info@skyhorsepublishing.com.

Sky Pony® is a registered trademark of Skyhorse Publishing, Inc.®,
a Delaware corporation.
Visit our website at www.skyponypress.com.

10 9 8 7 6 5 4 3 2 1

Library of Congress Cataloging-in-Publication Data is available on file.

Cover design by Brian Peterson
Book design by Joshua Barnaby

Print ISBN: 978-1-5107-2211-8
Ebook ISBN: 978-1-5107-2213-2

Printed in The United States of America

TABLE OF CONTENTS

INTRODUCTION

Since Pokémon GO was released in July of 2016, I've spent countless hours catching Pokémon and exploring its vast world, having fun and trying to figure out how the game works. Throughout my time playing the game, I've found a lot of neat tips and tricks to help me more catch more Pokémon, battle better, and learn how to master the game.

Anytime I visited a new neighborhood or city, I opened up Pokémon GO to see what monsters I could find. Anytime I had thirty minutes or an hour to spare, I would try to battle at new gyms and seek out new Pokémon. And anytime I was waiting in line at the store or the movies, I'd either be playing Pokémon or researching about Pokémon GO. It isn't necessarily reaching a certain level or catching more monsters than all the other players that makes you a master, but your ability to explore and learn more that makes you a highly-skilled Pokémon Go player.

But after all of my Pokémon GO playing, research, and hundreds of miles spent driving to find new Pokémon, there's one thing that has stuck out as the most important tip for becoming a Pokémon GO master: keep learning. There are always going to be new Pokémon to find, new battles to take part in, and new areas to explore, and it's up to you to learn from these experiences. There are going to always be players at higher levels than you who you can learn from, and new ones who just started the game who can learn from you. Most of the time I spent writing this book was when I was at Level Seventeen, where there were a lot of trainers above and below. There were a lot of achievements I still needed to accomplish and plenty more I had already done to that point. I'm above that level now, but with every trainer who was above me came an opportunity to find out something new, like which items I'd unlock at higher levels. And with every trainer who was below me I was given the chance to hone a basic skill I already knew, like how to throw a great curveball. There's always going be a trainer who's accomplished a bit more than you, no matter how many hours you put into the game. But your desire to learn, explore, and find new things in Pokémon GO will put you above the rest.

Follow my example and learn as much as you can when playing Pokémon GO. If you didn't successfully catch a monster, look back and ask why? If you won a tough gym battle, ask yourself why did you win this time and not other times. If you're in a new area or part of town, explore it and learn that much more about the game. That way, you'll be able to apply the tips and challenges in this book, and become a true Pokémon GO master.

—Justin Ryan

Pokémon GO is a fun game for anyone to play. There's lots of different monsters to catch, lots of PokéStops and areas to explore, and plenty of gyms for your Pokémon to battle it out with other trainers. There's plenty to learn in this fun, digital Pokémon world, and only with these tips, secrets, and challenges will you be able to become a true Pokémon master.

I'll have to move my feet if I want to battle this Raichu.

Rattata will be one of the many familiar faces you see in the game.

Before you start playing Pokémon GO, there are some questions you should answer. If you were defending a gym where there are a lot of fire-type Pokémon nearby, which type of Pokémon should you use? If you only had thirty minutes to play the game and were walking to a lot of different places, would it be better for you to use a lure or an incense to capture more Pokémon? If you had fifty of a certain Pokémon's Candy, would it be better to evolve that Pokémon, power it up, or neither? If you don't know the answers to these questions, don't worry, because after reading this guide, you'll be able to take on any battle or Pokémon this massive digital world throws at you.

A brand new,
newly-evolved Pidgeotto.

Vaporeon trying to make a late comeback in this battle against Flareon.

Each of these tips and challenges will help you out at certain points in the game, and will help in developing your skills as a trainer. Some pieces of information will help you catch Pokémon, others will help you navigate the map, some will show you how to unlock a PokéStop's true potential, and others will ensure your rise to victory in battles. It won't be easy, as the best Pokémon trainers have put in a lot of time and work to get where they are. But if there's one thing that's for sure, becoming a Pokémon GO master will be endless fun, and you'll have a great time on your Poke-journey.

1. HOW DOES THIS BOOK WORK?

Instead of being a guide to just the game, catching, or battling, this will focus on the individual tips for doing things in order to become a Pokémon master. These range from anything like how to catch a Pikachu as your starter Pokémon, how to evolve an Eevee into anything you wish, and advice to help you succeed in battle. This book is organized by tips and challenges.

An area with lots of powered-up PokéStops.

The Pokédex entry for the lovable Pikachu.

One of the many Medals you earn after achieving certain things in the game.

TIPS: are pieces are information that can help make a part of the game easier. If you're having trouble defeating an opponent or catching a certain type of Pokémon, or determining what type of Pokémon to leave defending a gym, this is where you would incorporate a tip from this book into the game.

Knowing when to use a lure is an example of a tip.

Learning to how to raise your own team's prestige at a gym is another one.

CHALLENGES: are things that you can strive to accomplish in the game to show off how good a Pokémon trainer you are. These include things like catching a hundred Pokémon, defeating ten gyms, and hatching a certain number of eggs in a certain amount of time. The point of these challenges is to serve as goals for yourself, to help you refine your skills as a trainer, and always give you new and exciting things to do in the game.

Learning a certain number of Pokémon to evolve would be considered a tip, like above with Nidoran becoming Nidorina.

HOW LONG WILL IT TAKE ME TO ACCOMPLISH THESE CHALLENGES/SECRETS?

There's a big, big world out there in Pokémon GO, you just have to take the time to explore it.

The short answer is a long time. The better answer is, it shouldn't matter. Pokémon GO, while offering over a hundred monsters to catch and endless battles to participate in, is ultimately a game where you need to find unique ways to keep yourself entertained. That's why you should always try new things, strive to catch new Pokémon, and fight in battles that will make you that much stronger as a competitor. This book will serve as a good guideline for unique ways to keep Pokémon GO a fun and challenging experience.

WHAT IF ONE TIP/CHALLENGE IS TOO HARD OR TAKES TOO LONG TO DO?

Catching all the Pokémon in this Sightings menu shouldn't take too long.

But catching five Pokémon before this incense runs out might be tough.

If you find yourself taking a long time to finish a challenge or incorporate a tip, just skip it and return to it later. You don't need to catch a hundred Pokémon to win five battles, and you don't need to hatch twenty eggs to explore twenty-five PokéStops. So feel free to mark down a challenge you want to accomplish later, or a tip you want to try out in the future. And then come back to it when you feel ready.

DO I NEED TO DO ONLY THE CHALLENGES IN THIS BOOK?

Not at all! Pokémon GO is a vast, wide world where you can accomplish anything, and if you do manage to complete everything in this book, there are still lots of things you can think of on your own to continue to make Pokémon GO as fun as possible. Did you collect every Pokémon there was? Good, now do it again! Have you claimed fifty different gyms in your team's name? Great job, now shoot for a hundred! It's up to you to think of fun ways to continue to make Pokémon GO a fun and rewarding experience.

You can think of your own challenges, too, like
how many times could I visit the same PokéStop
in one day?

Defeating your first Snorlax is one of the
most rewarding Pokémon GO experiences.

So what are you waiting for? There are Pokémon out
there to catch and battle! Grab your smartphone, open
Pokémon GO and embark on your journey to becoming a
Pokémon GO master!

SIGN UP FOR A POKÉMON GO TRAINER ACCOUNT

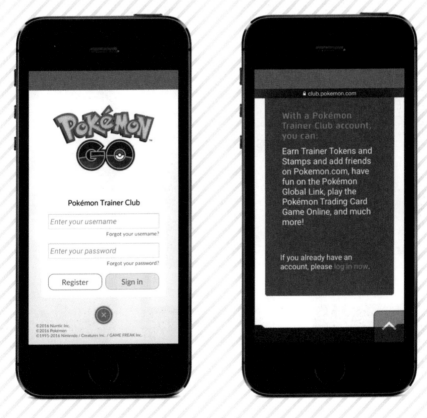

Here's what I see when I select the "sign up for a trainer account" option at the start screen.

If you have one of these accounts, you'll learn about new developments in Pokémon GO and to gain some great items when you're playing the game. Just make sure to remember your username password or keep it in a safe place, so if you ever need to log in again you'll have that ready.

PICK AN AWESOME OUTFIT AND THE BEST NAME FOR YOUR TRAINER

You can choose between these two.

And you can customize their appearance.

Just make sure you pick the best outfit possible before going on.

You have a lot of different choices on what clothes your trainer can wear, but you only have one chance to choose them. So make sure you take the time to get your trainer just perfect. Spend time looking at the different sweatshirts, hats, shoes, and more.

This nickname shows my enthusiasm for the game and how good of a Pokémon master I am.

You can also see what other trainers are named or what they chose to wear.

Pick a name that you like, something clever, inspiring, or funny. Some people name their trainers after their pets, and others after their favorite characters in movies or TV shows. Choose something really that means a lot to you, so that way you can show off your name at gyms and PokéStops.

3. GETTING STARTED

PICK WISELY BETWEEN BULBASAUR, SQUIRTLE, AND CHARMANDER.

You can see the adorable Charmander, Squirtle, and Bulbasaur circling around you. Picking one will be a tough choice!

These are the first Pokémon you encounter in the game, and while you can meet more of them later on, it's important you pick the right one for you to start off. Bulbasaur is the green monster, Charmander is the red one, and Squirtle is the blue one. Bulbasaur is weak to Charmander, Charmander is weak to Squirtle, and Squirtle isn't as strong against Bulbasaur. This only matters in battle. Just pick whichever one you like the most.

RENAME YOUR POKÉMON

I changed this guy's name to show off his electric personality.

Unlike your trainer, you can name and rename your Pokémon anytime you wish. Maybe name one after your pet, or a friend. I named one of my favorite Pokémon after my dog at home who has a similar color fur, so that way I'm reminded of him every time I play.

LEARN HOW TO LEVEL UP

You won't have to play long for your trainer to reach Level Two.

Leveling up is crucial to progressing in the game, and doing it the first time will give you an idea of what you need to do for each time after. Catch enough Pokémon and visit enough PokéStops, and quickly you'll find that you're now at Level Two.

The line in the middle near the bottom shows how much more XP I need to get to reach the next level.

If you select your trainer's picture in the bottom left corner, it'll tell you the amount of XP you have, and what you need to level up. This can help you set goals and things you need to do in order to get that amount to hit the next level. For example, if you only need two thousand XP, you can then plan to catch a lot of Pokémon, visit a few PokéStops, and maybe even battle at a few gyms to get that remaining amount. It can be frustrating when you're trying to get to that next level and even after hours of playing, you're still in the same spot. But knowing that number in the back of your head will help you set goals on what you need to do to advance. And having those goals in place and knowing the necessary things you need to do to reach that next level will make things easier.

EARN LOTS OF MEDALS

Medals come from achieving certain challenges in the game, like visiting a certain number of PokéStops or capturing a certain number of a type of Pokémon. They also give you some XP. You can see what Medals you've earned and set goals for yourself for those you need to earn by selecting your picture and scrolling down.

These Medals came from a lot of hard work, and there's still a lot more to earn.

4. CATCHING

CATCH A PIKACHU AS YOUR FIRST POKÉMON

Look, it's Pikachu!

Look, it's Pikachu! And Abra!

If you don't want Squirtle, Charmander, or Bulbasaur as your starter, you can have Pikachu simply by walking away from the three monsters and not having them in your view. Do this a few times and Pikachu should appear. Remember that all of the Pokémon can't be seen on your phone while doing this, and even after they disappear from view you'll have to keep walking a bit more until they respawn again. Even if you don't get this exactly right, you can still catch Pikachu later in the game, but this is how you can start off with him as your first Pokémon.

Pikachu after appearing
near Bulbasaur,
Charmander, and Squirtle.

Pikachu after getting
captured.

CATCH YOUR FIRST POKÉMON IN THE WILD

Pidgey will likely be one of the most common Pokémon you see in the wild.

It doesn't matter if it's a rare Pokémon or something more common, catching Pokémon is one of the main aspects of the game, and doing it the first time will teach you how a big bulk of the game operates. When you see a Pokémon appear on the map, select it, and then you'll be able to catch it just like you did for the starter. Early Pokémon probably aren't going to be anything special or rare—they'll likely be a Pidgey, Ekans, or something that is more commonly found in the wild. Just the act of catching one is one of the basic fundamentals of the game.

There's Pidgey right now!

Now I have to catch the bird before it leaves this sidewalk.

LEARN HOW TO THROW CURVEBALLS

You can tell it's a curveball if there are stars shooting out of the ball.

Curveballs are a bit harder than regular throws but they're worth it. Spin the ball when you're about to throw with your thumb, and when you finally do throw, it should curve. Time this correctly and you'll get an extra boost of XP. If you're throwing your curveball from the left, you'll want to aim it slightly more left, and if you're throwing it from the right, you'll want to aim it slightly more right. Or start from one of the bottom corners and move your way up and around the Pokémon to get your throw. Curveballs, are really just something that you can only learn by practicing them as often as possible within the game. It'll be difficult at first, but when you finally have the right maneuver down for throwing curveballs, they'll be easy as pie.

USE RAZZ BERRIES TO HELP CATCH A DIFFICULT POKÉMON

This Paras, although a common Pokémon, has a pretty high CP, so I want to use a Razz Berry here.

Razz Berries make catching easier. Simply use one before your throw, and it should increase your chances of catching that monster if your throw is successful. These don't work all the time, as you can still end up with a Pokémon running away. And a lot of times, your throw won't be successful, or the Pokémon will break free from your Poké Ball, requiring you to start the process all over again. You just need to keep using them whenever you get a chance and they will help making catching any Pokémon easier.

KNOW WHEN TO USE A STRONGER BALL VS. A WEAKER

I'm going to switch out a regular Poké Ball for a Master Ball to catch this Rattata.

If you're trying to catch a Pidgey with 10 CP, you're fine with a regular Poké Ball. But if you're going after an Ivysaur with a 350 CP, it'd be better to use a more powerful ball like a Great or Ultra Ball. Sometimes you'll only have Great Balls when a regular Poké Ball would have done fine. And other times you'll desperately wish you had an Ultra Ball to use on a Pokémon you wanted badly, and all you had was a regular Poké Ball. Just try to keep your weaker balls for weaker Pokémon. The stronger balls only come after you've reached certain levels in the game, so keep advancing to get ahold of them.

KNOW WHEN TO RUN FROM A CATCHING ATTEMPT

And I've got plenty of Geodudes already, but not nearly enough balls to capture Pokemon I really want.

I've given this Paras a Razz Berry and already threw one Master Ball and missed. But really, is it worth it to catch this Pokémon?

You don't have to try to catch every Pokémon you see. If you're low on Poké Balls, or if you decide to focus on other Pokémon, or for any other reason, just hit the run button in the top left corner. And if you change your mind right after running away, that Pokémon still might be on your map, so you can try catching them again. Sometimes you may not even want to catch any Pokémon during the game, you'll just want to battle, or visit a few PokéStops, and a monster will appear in front of you. Keep your eye on whatever your goal is and if you find yourself trying to catch a Pokémon you don't want, just walk away.

VISIT NEW AREAS TO FIND NEW POKÉMON

There's more than just these PokéStops in the game, I need to keep moving to find more.

Immediately around me, I can see that there's very little Pokémon or PokéStops to be found on this map, but if I move just a little bit, there's a lot more going on.

Just playing the game in your neighborhood will only give you so many opportunities to catch different Pokémon. Visit new areas to discover different monsters. People find different types of Pokémon by visiting areas they had never been to, like water Pokémon at the beach, or rock and ground based Pokémon while hiking different trails. Plus, sitting in the same old spot can get boring, so this is a good reason for you to explore. You won't always be able to get up and go explore somewhere new, but doing so whenever possible will bring you a much more diverse crowd of monsters.

UTILIZE THE SIGHTINGS MENU EFFECTIVELY

There's a good amount of Pokémon I haven't seen before, because only their shadows appear here. So I think it's worth it to stay and find them.

The Sightings menu is helpful when telling you certain monsters are in your area. Look at it to get a general idea of what Pokémon might be in your area. Follow the rustling leaves for a chance at finding Pokémon, but don't waste hours trying to find one that may have disappeared.

Just because there are certain Pokémon listed in the Sightings menu doesn't mean those will be the only Pokémon that show up there. And just because those Pokémon are in the menu doesn't mean they'll even appear. The Sightings menu is a good suggestion but by no means a comprehensive guide to finding new monsters. Keep it as an idea of what Pokémon are there in your area to catch, but always continue to explore to find new Pokémon.

Here, though, there aren't any Pokémon I actually want in the Sightings menu.

I spent hours trying to catch a Squirtle that appeared in the Sightings menu once and it never actually showed up. Always keep moving; don't spend too long in the same location, otherwise you might just see the same old Pokémon over and over again.

DON'T GET DISAPPOINTED IF YOU DON'T CATCH A PARTICULAR POKÉMON

I really wanted this Ponyta but it got away.

Not catching a Pokémon you really wanted isn't fun, but the game will give you more opportunities to find that Pokémon later on. It may not appear right away, or even a week later, but if you continue looking for that Pokémon you will find it again. You can only do so much to try and catch a particular Pokémon, so don't get down on yourself if you don't find it. Plus, certain Pokémon can be better found in certain areas, so focus your search and that will give you a better chance to catch them.

READ CP TO DETERMINE IF THE POKÉMON IS WORTH HAVING

The fact that this Pokémon's CP isn't listed makes me want to catch it even more.

CP is a good indicator not only of how strong that Pokémon is now but also how strong it may become. If you have twenty Pidgeys in your collection but come across a Pidgey with a very high CP, it's worth it to catch that one, even though you have many already. Plus, catching any Pokémon, no matter how rare or common, or weak or strong, will raise XP and help you level up faster. If you come across a certain Pokémon with a low CP, and you already have enough Candy of its kind in your stock and don't want to take the time catching it, then don't.

KEEP A STEADY SUPPLY OF BALLS

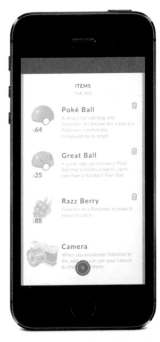

I have plenty of Poké Balls, could use a few more Great Balls, but for the most part I'm in good shape.

I have more than enough Great Balls to catch this Geodude

You don't want to be caught not having enough Poké Balls when you discover your favorite Pokémon. And then when you go to buy more from the shop or collect more from PokéStops, the monster has disappeared. Keep track of how many Poké Balls you have on you at all times. If you're running low, visit more PokéStops, or even buy some from the shop if you have a parent's permission. Poké Balls are essentially the most important item in the game: you need them to catch Pokémon, and you need to catch Pokémon in order to battle them. So if you don't have any Poké Balls that all falls apart. You'll want to keep a solid track of how many items you have and need at all times, but Poké Balls should be at the top of your list.

LEARN HOW TO DISTINGUISH BETWEEN GOOD AREAS TO FIND POKÉMON

Places like shopping malls, gas stations, or really any place with a lot of people around are good spots to find Pokémon. Famous landmarks or mountains or beaches are good too, in order to find water, rock, and dragon types. Look at your map to see where a lot of PokéStops are in one area, and that's a good place to start exploring. On this map, you can see a swarm of different PokéStops, some powered up by lures, but literally there are PokéStops on every different corner. This park, seen below, is a great place to catch Pokémon, as there were lots of people playing the game and PokéStops not too far away with lures out. I can keep going from one stop to the next to get new items and see new monsters.

Two gyms nearby with a few PokéStops in the area tells me this is a good spot to look for Pokémon.

Other good areas to find Pokémon are those that have lots of streets, lots of PokéStops, and lots of people around to power up those PokéStops. Pay attention to these types of areas when looking on the map, and even try to think of some on your own a little further away that might be good places to find Pokémon. Chances are, you'll probably be right.

PERFECT YOUR SHOT

I'm about to make direct contact with this Pokémon.

It's one of the things you'll be doing most often in the game but also one of the hardest to do correctly. Practice your shot and practice catching as much as you can. Know how to hit your Pokémon perfectly and how to time your shots just right. You'll need to learn your own finger technique and strength, and how to throw a ball closer to you, and how to throw one further away. You'll also need to learn how long it actually takes for your ball to make contact with the Pokémon, and you'll need to pay attention to when the Pokémon moves or jumps. And this'll also help you understand more about the circles that appear for each monster, and how you can plan to catch them better by throwing and using Berries.

KNOW THE RINGS

A green, medium-to-large ring tells me this Pikachu will be easy to catch but may pose a few difficulties if I don't throw correctly.

And I'm able to this this Geodude with no problem.

A green circle means a Pokémon is easier to catch, orange or yellow means it's more difficult, and red means hardest. A small circle also means that Pokémon is easier to catch, while a big circle means it's harder. If you hold your ball, you can notice the circles start bigger and then gradually become smaller. When they're small, this is when you should throw the ball. You don't always need to make a really strong effort with the rings to catch a Pokémon though. Sometimes all you'll need to do is just throw and before you know it, the Pokémon will be yours. In those situations when you're going after a difficult Pokémon, pay attention to these circles, as they'll also help you determine if you need to use a different ball or even a Razz Berry.

VISIT DIFFERENT PHYSICAL LOCATIONS TO SEE NEW POKÉMON

The first time you see a Lapras in the field or at a gym may be when you're near a body of water, like an ocean or pond.

The beach is a great place to catch water Pokémon, and the mountains a great place to catch rock Pokémon. At churches you can find lots of fairy Pokémon, and at stadiums lots of fighting Pokémon. Go to different, specific physical locations to find different, specific type of monsters. You'll still need cellular reception to play the game, and that oftentimes can be lost when you're in a remote area. But moving around and exploring will reveal different types.

5. CATCHING CHALLENGES

CATCH FIVE POKÉMON OUTSIDE OF YOUR IMMEDIATE AREA

Onix only appeared when I went outside my regular map.

It's easy to get into a habit of just catching Pokémon in your nearby vicinity. Get up and explore a different area with a trusted adult, and catch five new Pokémon there. They don't have to be rare or super-powered Pokémon. This is a way for you to learn more about a different area, get some good exercise, and also improve your throwing skills. Take pictures of each monster that you capture so you can keep track of all the cool places you visited and all the interesting Pokémon that you've seen along the way. If you're having a really fun time catching during this challenge, keep going! See how much you can catch outside your immediate area in a certain amount of time.

To make this more interesting, you could target only powerful Pokémon with high CP levels. The great thing about catching Pokémon is that you often have multiple attempts to throw a ball, so even if your first attempt doesn't work, you can throw another. Catching a high powered Pokémon, though, is a difficult task, and doing so on only one shot is even more challenging. This will help refine your throwing techniques and learn just how useful those circles around a Pokémon can be. It'll also teach you to wait for the right moment to throw, since Pokémon have a nasty habit of moving around during the catching process. You can still use a Razz Berry for this challenge, but the point of it is to master your throwing skills, so when you finally meet that Pokémon you've been dying to catch, you'll be ready.

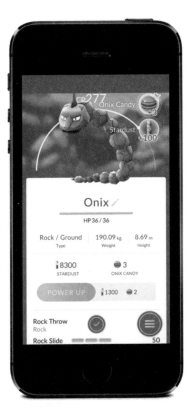

I now finally have
Onix in my collection.

CATCH ONE OF EACH TYPE OF POKÉMON

Those shadows of Pokémon on the bottom mean that I still need to catch those types.

Not only is this a good challenge to get you used to catching Pokémon, but will also help boost the diversity in your collection. You'll be way ahead in the game if you have one of each of these types: Fire, Water, Grass, Electric, Rock, Ground, Flying, Poison, Ghost, Dragon, Fighting, Normal, Psychic, Bug, Ice, and Fairy. It'll also help when you're getting ready for battle. If this challenge is proving too difficult, you can also try to hatch different types instead of just catching them. If this is too easy, try catching two of each type of Pokémon in a certain amount of time.

COLLECT ALL OF ONE TYPE OF POKÉMON

Sandshrew is just waiting to be caught.

I am well on my way to catching all of the Rock-type Pokémon.

There's a lot of fire-type Pokémon, a lot of water-type, and so on. But it isn't impossible to collect all of one type. This is a good way to prove that you have dedication as a trainer, and you can also show off to others all of the fire types, water types, or whatever other type you choose to catch. If you're in specific area where a lot of one type of Pokémon hang out, like a beach for water Pokémon, that might be helpful in catching certain types. Even though I've encountered lots of grass Pokémon where I live, it took me a while to actually encounter all, or a decent portion, of them. This challenge will give you an idea of what is needed to catch Pokémon, while also helping you learn where to find them.

CATCH ONE OF EACH POKÉMON IN THE SIGHTINGS MENU

There is one Pidgey and one Rattata in this vicinity, so I'd only need to catch one Pidgey and one Rattata to succeed at this challenge.

This is hard, since a lot of Pokémon appear and then disappear. But it isn't impossible with the help of lures, incenses, and just plain old luck. Even if you don't succeed at this challenge, it's a good way for you to learn how to locate monsters quickly. The fact is that all of the monsters in the Sightings menu can be caught—they won't always be caught, but they can be. So try your best to catch them all.

COLLECT A HUNDRED DIFFERENT POKÉMON

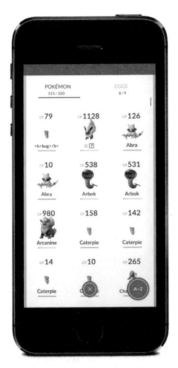

You may want to catch Pokémon that are more rare, but it's still worth it to go after common ones.

Getting your first Pidgey is where you start off to Pokémon GO greatness.

This can be done by catching and evolving Pokémon you already have, but the point of this challenge is to catch one hundred and show the time required to get a lot of Pokémon. And to discover the different places you'll have to go to get a lot of different varieties. This challenge can take a day or a week, but it's necessary to help you become a true Pokémon Master with a solid collection of Pokémon behind you. If you want to make it really exciting, you can try to accomplish this challenge in a certain amount of time. The point is to help you locate which types of Pokémon you want more quickly, and to raise your catching skills.

CATCH EVERY POKÉMON

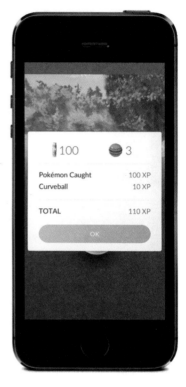

I've captured and seen a lot of Pokémon, but there's still a long way to go to catching them all.

You'll see this screen over and over again, but just remember each new Pokémon you capture puts you that much closer to getting them all.

It's supposedly been done before, and there's no reason why you can't do it. Know where certain Pokémon hide, know how to evolve your Pokémon, and play as much as you can. Over a hundred Pokémon and then some sounds like a lot of hard work, and there are some that supposedly can only be found in certain parts of the world. Know which areas to go to, hatch a lot of eggs, catch a lot of Pokémon, and it is possible. This is the second most important thing you'll need to do in order to become a Pokémon Master.

6. UTILIZING THE MAP

USE THE COMPASS TO KEEP YOURSELF GROUNDED

It's easy to get lost on the map, and also in real life, when playing the game. Use the compass to help keep track of wherever you are. The red arrow is always pointing north, and the arrow beneath it is south. Taking a break from the game just to get a clear grasp of your surroundings is helpful, especially if you're exploring in an area that is new to you and easy to get lost in.

There's a lot of activity and streets on this map, so I use the compass to help keep track of where I am.

ZOOM IN/ZOOM OUT TO GET A BETTER VIEW OF THINGS

As you can see, zooming out on the bottom screen gives me a much bigger view of what's happening, while zooming in gets me up close in the action.

Sometimes we only think there's so much on a map because we're looking at a smaller view of it. Zoom out on your map and use different angles so you can get a better understanding of the gyms and PokéStops nearby. I've often overlooked PokéStops or gyms that I could have walked to because I wasn't using the full potential of zooming in or out on the map. And other times, I thought that there was nothing worthwhile near me until I actually zoomed out and saw that there were some great gyms and PokéStops I wanted to visit nearby. This way you'll be able to see everything there is to on the map.

PLAN YOUR MAP TRAVELS IN ADVANCE

There's so much I want to see on this map, but
I should pick a good route to accomplish it all.

If there's a new part of the map you want to explore
but you only have an hour to do so, it's best to plan out
where you want to go ahead of time to maximize your
trip. Know which PokéStops you want to visit, which
gyms you want to battle at, and the best paths to get
from one location to the other. Know whether there are
bike paths, or if the area is going to be busy, with a lot
of people in the way. Also, if there are any interesting
landmarks you want to see or PokéStops that are catching your eye. You'll get more from your journey than
just wandering around without a specific goal. Plan out
in your head which streets you want to explore.

BUT ALSO LEAVE SOME ROOM FOR SPONTANEITY

It might be fun just to wander this map for a while.

A lot of the fun from the game comes from exploring new areas, and part of that is exploring parts you didn't plan to. So while it's good to have a plan, it's also good to give yourself time to go wherever you feel at that moment. If you have an hour to spend playing Pokémon GO in a new location, spend forty-five minutes of that time exploring a planned out route, and the other fifteen set aside for you to check out places you didn't originally intend to. Some of the best monsters that players have caught, and the best gym battles they've found themselves in, have been at those locations where they didn't originally plan on going.

7. EXPLORING POKÉSTOPS

VISIT YOUR FIRST POKÉSTOP

This is what a PokéStop looks like when you approach it.

This will give you an idea of how PokéStops work. Your first PokéStop could be five feet away from you or a longer walk down the street. But visiting your first will help you understand how PokéStops will help your trainer out the most. When you're at your first PokéStop, swipe on the image to spin it, revealing items that are lurking behind. Touch them to pick them up. You have to wait five minutes until you can claim more items from the same PokéStop. But doing this will give you an idea of how a major component of the game will work.

USE A LURE MODULE AT A POKÉSTOP

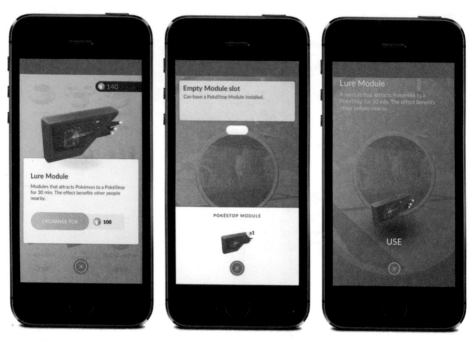

I bought a lure in the shop and now I'm going to use it at this PokéStop.

Using a lure module means that a PokéStop will attract Pokémon for thirty minutes. You'll have to be near the PokéStop to gain its effects. It's also a helpful way to meet players in real life since all players benefit from a lure: they'll be able to see that same PokéStop powered up on their own Pokémon GO game as you, and chances are you'll see the same types of Pokémon appear at that PokéStop. You can get these lure modules by collecting them in the game or by purchasing them in the shop.

USE AN INCENSE

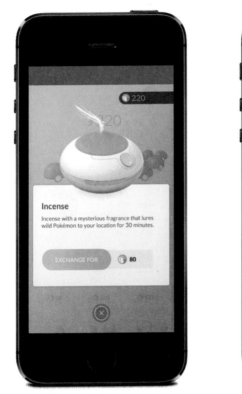

I bought an incense in the shop and immediately started using it in the game.

If you're trying to catch Pokémon while moving around, an incense might be a better way to go, as it'll follow you around, wherever you go. Remember, an incense only helps your own trainer, so even if you're walking next to another trainer in real life who's playing the game, the incense will only work on you. If you're walking with a friend somewhere and you're both playing Pokémon GO, it might be a good idea for both of you to use incenses at the same time so you can both catch a lot of Pokémon, although the monsters that appear for each of you may be different.

KNOW WHEN IT'S WORTH IT TO USE A LURE MODULE

There are so many PokéStops to power up a lure with, and I like this one closest to me.

Are you going to be at that same spot for thirty minutes? Or are you going to be going to different places? If you're going stay still, then it's best to use a lure module, because you'll want the whole amount of time to use it. For the maximum effect, you should commit to using the lure. For example, if you're at the movies and there's a PokéStop right outside, it probably wouldn't be worth it to use a lure since you'll have to put your phone away in the theater. Even if you use a lure and have to take a break for a few minutes, that still gives you a solid twenty-five minutes to catch Pokémon with it. You don't have to be plugged into your phone every second while using a lure, but spend as much time as you can catching Pokémon.

KNOW WHEN IT'S WORTH IT TO USE AN INCENSE

And here I can see a PokéStop with a lure far away, but I know I won't be able to walk over there, so it's better to use an incense here.

I know I'm going to be moving a lot and will have time to catch Pokémon, so I'll want to use an incense.

Are you going to be walking around with your family in a new area, where you'll have a lot of opportunities to play the game for thirty minutes? Or is your phone going to be in your pocket the whole time? If you're moving and know you'll be able to have your phone out, that is the best time to use an incense. But if you're going to be going on a hike and want to pay attention to the nature around you, you probably won't want to use an incense, even though you'll be moving around a lot. Time flies quickly in Pokémon GO and in real life, and you'll find sometimes watching hours go by like minutes just because you're having so much fun. This is why you always need to pay attention to whether incenses are the right item to use.

HOW TO DECIDE BETWEEN LURE AND INCENSE

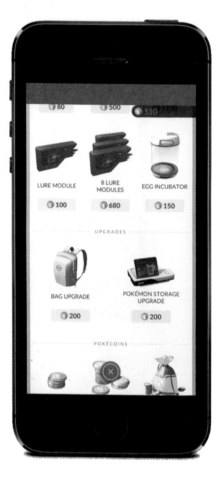

One thing to keep in mind is
that lures are more expensive
in the shop than incense.

Lures are better if you're standing still, while incenses are better if you're moving around. An incense can still work if you're in the same spot, but it's best used when you're exploring new areas. Both help make more Pokémon appear near you, so an incense could still be helpful even if you're in the same spot, or a lure, even if you leave that PokéStop for three minutes and come back right after. But as a general rule, use lures if you're staying put, and incense if you're moving around.

READ THE INFORMATION BEHIND A POKÉSTOP

Here's an interesting historical tidbit I learned from this PokéStop right here. I've been down that street many times before but never knew about that until I read this PokéStop.

PokéStops have more to them than just items and lures. They're places where you can learn more about your city and cool landmarks. Always check out the information PokéStops have to offer, some might even have interesting stories or jokes. I learned a lot about the city I live in by visiting different PokéStops and reading the information there, there's a lot of cool stuff you can find out!

KNOW WHAT THOSE FLOATING PETALS MEAN

This PokéStop has been
powered with a lure.

This is a PokéStop that has a lure on it. If you don't
see the floating petals, it means that it's just a regular
PokéStop. You can't power up a PokéStop that already
has a lure on it, you'll have to wait for that lure to run
out until you can use another one again. If you don't
know when a PokéStop was powered up, you can safely
assume that there is less than thirty minutes left on the
lure. If you do ever see a PokéStop with floating petals,
which you will and often, just go there and start taking
part in all the Pokémon catching and item grabbing fun.

PAY ATTENTION TO THE CLOCK ON AN INCENSE

I looked away from Pokémon GO for what felt like a second, and when I came back, I saw I had already lost five minutes on my incense.

It's easy to get distracted catching Pokémon with a lure and not even realize how much time you have left. Always keep track of the clock ticking in the lure corner so you have a good idea of when it'll expire. If you want to start an incense for thirty minutes but need to do something that takes ten minutes, it might be better to do that task first and then start the incense, so you'll have that full amount of time to catch Pokémon.

PAY ATTENTION TO THE THINGS THAT POP UP UNDERNEATH POKÉMON

I'm using both an incense and a lure right now, but the purple rings under Eevee tell me that it appeared because of a lure.

Here you can clearly see this Abra appeared because of my incense.

If you see a Pokémon appear with purple smoke underneath it, that means it was attracted to your incense. If it appears with purple rings, it was attracted to your lure. If nothing appears, it spawned under normal circumstances. This'll give you a good idea of how effective the items are for you. You might notice different results each time you use the items, so keep track of which monsters are appearing more often because of lures or because of the incense.

VISIT NEW AREAS TO FIND NEW POKÉSTOPS

A PokéStop in the Southern California area.

A PokéStop at an historic theater in Los Angeles area.

Go to the beach, take a hike in the mountains, visit a different shopping mall on the other side of town. Only by going to new areas will you find all of the different Pokémon waiting to be captured and the PokéStops that can give you more items. Plus, visiting as many as possible will help you unlock more Medals in the game.

RETRIEVE AS MANY ITEMS FROM POKÉSTOPS AS POSSIBLE

Three to four Poké Balls and one to two potions doesn't seem like much at first at a PokéStop. But keep visiting them often and those items quickly add up.

Spinning a PokéStop will give you items, and then you'll have to wait five minutes until you can get more. If you'll be near the same PokéStop for fifteen minutes or more, keep track of how long it's been since you've spun the PokéStop so you know exactly when to go back to get new items. If there's more than one PokéStop in your immediate area, you could visit all of them quickly and get even more items.

DON'T FORGET TO GRAB ITEMS

I only got a few Poké Balls from this PokéStop, but I'll be here for a while so I can get even more later on.

It'd be unfortunate to realize you didn't grab these even after you visited the PokéStop.

It's easy to forget to actually pick up the items after you've swiped a PokéStop. Make sure you click on each one so you don't potentially lose out on those items because they disappear. Sure, it's only a five-minute wait to have to swipe that PokéStop again, but you don't want to lose any items you could have had in the meantime, especially if you've been waiting to collect Poké Balls to catch more Pokémon or use potions or Revives to heal your monsters.

DON'T USE A LURE OR INCENSE WHEN YOU DON'T HAVE THE TIME

I know I'll have to stop playing the game in ten minutes, so using a lure or an incense would be a waste.

And I'm about to close out of the game for a while here, so the incense was essentially worthless.

Lures and incense are helpful but you don't want to waste them by using them when you don't need to. Only use them when you know you'll have thirty minutes to spare when playing the game. If you want to be nice, you could use a lure at a PokéStop for other people to use, but remember you only have a certain amount of these, and you'll have to find more in the game or buy them in the shop if you want to continue using them.

DON'T SPEND TOO MUCH ON LURES OR INCENSES AT THE SHOP

Here I have only 140 coins, and it may not be worth it to buy lures or incense.

Spending $1 or $5 on PokéCoins doesn't seem like much, but it can quickly add up.

You can get lures or incenses any time you want in the shop, but that doesn't mean you should. These items are easily found in the wild, and it isn't worth the money to buy PokéCoins just to get these items. Spending $1 to buy a lure may not seem like a lot, but that money can quickly add up. It's generally best to challenge yourself to find these in the game.

DON'T UNDERVALUE THE POWER OF LURES

I only see a Caterpie here now, but there's bound to be more Pokémon later.

This PokéStop is in an area with lots of people around, and if I use a lure on it, it's bound to bring a lot of Pokémon.

Lures, simply put, bring up more Pokémon than you would have normally seen just playing the game. Even if there's a PokéStop with a lure that's a bit away from your house, it still might be worth going there to see what Pokémon are in that area. Lures won't guarantee a rare Pokémon will appear or that you can catch fifteen new monsters in 30 minutes, but they will make more monsters appear than normally would have.

BUT DON'T OVERESTIMATE THEM EITHER

This area doesn't really have much stuff going on for Pokémon GO, so even if I do use a lure or incense, it probably won't do much.

This Growlithe just showed up on its own, it didn't need a lure or incense.

You can use lures and incenses all day long and still not catch that one Pokémon you've been really wanting. Again, the best way to find new Pokémon is to visit new areas, and at the end of the day, lures and incenses can only do so much. If you're in a new area for a short amount of time and there are a lot of PokéStops to see but only one powered by a lure, go visit the other PokéStops and then come back to see if there's anything worthwhile at the powered-up one.

ONLY DOUBLE DOWN IF YOU HAVE A STEADY SUPPLY OF BOTH

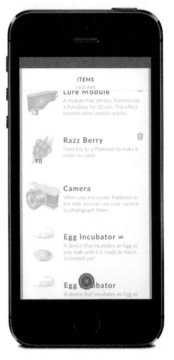

I had enough lures and incenses in my stock to use both without being wasteful.

I only have three lures in my inventory, so it wouldn't be a good idea to double down on them.

Lures and incenses don't cancel each other out when used together, although you don't necessarily see a massive amount of Pokémon when you use both, either. I've noticed just a slight increase in the number of Pokémon I'd see if I had only used one. The best time to use both at the same time is when you have a healthy amount in your items collection. Otherwise you wouldn't want to run out and then suddenly want to use a lure or incense.

DON'T GET HOOKED TO JUST ONE POKÉSTOP

None of these PokéStops are powered up, but they're all full of potential.

That PokéStop in the center is one of my favorites, but I need to keep seeing more to keep things exciting.

Sure, it's easy and convenient to just get new items and use lures on the local PokéStop over and over again. But you can only get certain Medals in the game and achieve more by visiting other PokéStops. Not even as an achievement but just for fun. It's cool to go to different PokéStops, look at the information behind each one, and learn a little bit more about your town or area. That one favorite PokéStop of yours will most likely always be there. Go out and explore all the other ones you aren't normally able to.

DON'T GET CONSUMED WITH POWERED-UP POKÉSTOPS

There are three powered-up PokéStops here that caught my attention, but really I just want to battle at this gym.

None of these PokéStops are powered up, but they're all full of potential.

It's definitely exciting to see three PokéStops with lures in one central area, but you can soon find yourself spending an hour or two in the same spot, whereas you could have caught a lot more Pokémon of different types or have battled at different gyms had you kept moving. Staying put in one place will take away from the fun of the game, even if there are power-ups. Exploring should always be a top priority.

RIDE IN A CAR TO FIND NEW POKÉSTOPS

I won't necessarily be able to get to these PokéStops all in one night, so I'll have a trusted adult take me to see them.

Cars, buses, and subways can transport you to different areas where you can find Pokémon. If you're in a car, make sure a responsible adult is driving while you check out all the monsters speeding by you. If you're riding a bus or train, take note of all the Pokémon appearing, but also make sure you still get off at the right stop. Just like you need to pay attention when you're walking and playing Pokémon GO, so does whoever is driving you in a car. Since you'll probably be asking to pull over at different places, gyms and PokéStops, they'll still need to be paying attention to the road. If there are a lot of kids at your school or in your neighborhood who play Pokémon GO, see if you can get a trusted adult to do a Pokémon GO-caravan, where you get to explore as your driver has some fun, too.

8. POKÉSTOP CHALLENGES

TRAVEL TO FIVE POKÉSTOPS OUTSIDE YOUR IMMEDIATE AREA

F. SCOTT WILSON DEDICATION TABLET

Yosemite Recreation Center, Eagle Rock.

I had to go a few miles away from my neighborhood to find this PokéStop.

Just like it's important to catch five Pokémon outside of your immediate area, it's important to visit five PokéStops as well. This way you can discover new parts of your town or city you didn't know about, and get a more diverse range of items, and maybe catch a bigger pool of Pokémon. Remember to read the information at each stop, and keep note of any possible ones you might want to use a lure on. This challenge will help get you in shape for all the walking around you'll do while playing.

CATCH FIVE POKÉMON IN THIRTY MINUTES WITH A LURE MODULE

Even if a Pokémon appears because of a lure, you can still use Razz Berries to increase your chances of catching it.

Lures bring a lot of Pokémon to you, and this challenge will help you master being able to get the most out of a PokéStop when it's powered up. Catch five, no matter what CP or type. This way you can get better at catching in short time requirements, and also get a good idea of what Pokémon will appear at that particular PokéStop and how often. If your PokéStop is at a business or in a public location, something like a library or a restaurant, see if they'll let you sit and play for a while as you capture monsters. Chances are you'll notice other people joining in.

CATCH THREE WHILE USING INCENSE

I just started with this incense and have more than enough time to catch Pokémon.

You'll have to walk around a bit to get a good mix of Pokémon, but being able to capture three while using an incense will help teach you how to stay active while catching Pokémon in short periods of time. This challenge will give you a good idea of what Pokémon you see when you're using incense, as well as how frequently they appear in the wild, and how much you traveled in order to attract them. To make this challenge even more interesting, see how far you can travel in the first fifteen minutes of the incense and then return. Chances are, you traveled back faster than you went out. Next time you do this, see if you can travel an even greater distance in those fifteen minutes, while capturing more and more Pokémon each different time you do it. You can do this while walking or running in a safe area like an open field or track, not necessarily by the side of a road or on a sidewalk. You can also try this while riding in the car as a family member drives, just as long as they are driving safely.

CATCH TEN WHILE USING BOTH

A Great Ball after catching a
Pokémon while using a lure.

You'll need thirty minutes to do this, but it'll be worth it.
Find a PokéStop where you can move freely about the
area, someplace preferably in a field or park, not necessarily near a crowded street. Use both items and stay
within distance of the lure while still moving around.
You can even move away from the PokéStop where
the lure is powered, but the end goal is to catch ten
Pokémon before thirty minutes run out. If you accomplish this challenge, set more for yourself: catch fifteen
Pokémon before time runs out for both, catch twenty
Pokémon using both but at different moments, catch
ten different types of Pokémon while using both at the
same time.

9. EVOLVING/ POWERING UP POKÉMON

KNOW WHEN AND WHEN NOT TO EVOLVE

I can evolve this Pidgey right now if I want to, but it might be better to wait.

Let's say you just captured a Pokémon and have enough Candy to evolve it. If you want to gain the XP and don't want to power up any other of that Pokémon, then it's a good idea to evolve. But if you have a Pokémon with a low CP and you're saving its Candy to power up another of that Pokémon, then evolving wouldn't be a good idea. I have plenty of Pidgeys, a few Pidgeottos and more than enough Pidgey Candy to evolve them. But I also know that I'm rarely going to use Pidgeot in battle and when I do, it'll only be because I can't use any of my stronger or more favored Pokémon. Still, evolving a Pidgey just to gain XP wouldn't hurt at all, I'm not really going to use that Pidgey Candy for anything else, and I'm not using Stardust to evolve it. Evolving is fun but it isn't always the best scenario, so ask yourself what you're trying to get out of evolving and if it's the best course for you.

KNOW WHEN AND WHEN NOT TO POWER UP

Powering up Electabuzz might be a good idea, but I should check if there's any other Pokémon I want to power up first.

Let's say you have a Pokémon with a high CP that you want to make even more powerful. But then you remember you've been collecting that Pokémon's Candy so you can finally evolve another of it into its final form. It wouldn't be a good idea to power up here, especially considering that each power up requires Stardust, and you have less and less after each power up. You should power up if you know that specific Pokémon has the highest CP potential, that you have enough Candy to evolve too if need be, or that you won't want to use Stardust that could've been used on a more worthwhile Pokémon. While some Pokémon are rarer and more powerful than others, any Pokémon can be a true contender in battle if it's powered up enough, so don't be afraid to power up Pokémon you wouldn't have thought to on first glance. Just remember how much Candy you have to power up the ones you really want to.

DON'T LOSE TRACK OF YOUR CANDY

I could have sworn I had more Eevee Candy to power up Vaporeon, but I used a lot of it to evolve other Eevees.

When you get into the groove of catching Pokémon, you don't often think about how much of that Pokémon's Candy you already have, and sometimes you can look at your Pokémon list and see that you could have evolved it a day or two ago but you weren't paying attention. Keep a good idea of how much Candy you have for specific Pokémon you want to evolve or power up, and keep track even of those you aren't going to use for battle, since that Candy will help your Pokémon evolve, and help you gain XP and level up more quickly. Just like using too much Stardust, sometimes you might regret not evolving a Pokémon when you used its Candy to power up, or powering up a Pokémon when you should have used its Candy to evolve. Don't worry too much about what you already used your Candy on, and focus more on how you want to use your Candy in the future.

DON'T BE AFRAID TO TRANSFER POKÉMON BACK TO PROFESSOR WILLOW

Transferring is a necessary process to get Candy to evolve Pokémon.

It's rewarding to look at all the different Pokémon in your collection and think back on all the hard work you put into catching them. At the same time, you'll want to transfer over a lot of these extras to Professor Willow so you can get Candy for each type. Plus, this helps in the situation of finally being able to catch that monster you've wanted forever but aren't able to because you're already at the limit of how many Pokémon you can carry. Transferring can sometimes seem like it isn't really doing that much, since you're only getting one Candy and often times you'll need dozens more just to evolve your Pokémon. But literally every Candy you get from transferring is one Candy that you didn't have before, and that much more helpful to evolving and powering up Pokémon, and helping you succeed in the game. Just don't transfer the ones with high CP, only transfer the weaker ones.

KEEP TRACK OF WHICH POKÉMON YOU WANT TO EVOLVE

I know I'll want to evolve that Caterpie with the highest CP once I get enough Candy.

And I have a lot of Clefairys, but need to be careful which one I evolve.

Chances are you're going to end up with a lot of Pokémon in your collection and it can be hard to keep track of which ones you want to evolve or power up. Organizing your Pokémon list by CP or even by nick-naming specific Pokémon will be useful so you know specifically which ones you want to devote the time and resources into making as strong as possible. Evolving Pokémon of any type will help raise XP, and really will help you collect as many Pokémon as possible, but there are some Pokémon whose evolving should be more of a priority than others.

EARN A LOT OF STARDUST AND KEEP TRACK OF IT

I gained two hundred more Stardust in between catching this Paras and Dratini.

Stardust is the magical item that'll make your Pokémon stronger and better at battle. And the only way to get it is by catching Pokémon, hatching eggs, or defending gyms. So you'll have to play the game a lot to get Stardust to power up your Pokémon, and you'll also want to keep good track of how much you're using. Always ask yourself if it's worth it to power up this specific Pokémon, and if not, think of a better Pokémon to power up, or even just save your Stardust until that better Pokémon comes around. There are going to be times though when you regret using your Stardust on one Pokémon when you could have used it on another, or when you find yourself really wanting to power up a Pokémon but won't have the amount you need. This is why you should keep a careful eye on your Stardust, and if you ever need more, keep doing the things that will help you bring in more.

10. EVOLVING CHALLENGES

EVOLVE AN EEVEE INTO ANYTHING YOU WANT

You can pick which Pokemon your Eevee evolves into.

Usually, you don't have a choice for what Pokémon you get when Eevee evolves. The possible three options are Vaporeon, Flareon, and Jolteon, but if you don't do this trick, it'll be random which one you end up with. Here's what to do if you want to evolve Eevee into one of those three specific monsters:

If you want a Jolteon, nickname your Eevee "Sparky"

If you want a Flareon, nickname your Eevee "Pyro"

If you want a Vaporeon, nickname your Eevee "Rainer"

Here's Vaporeon and Jolteon battling.

And my Flareon is one of my favorites in my collection.

Then watch as your Eevee evolves into whichever Pokémon you chose. This is a good way to then have all three of these in your collection. The reason why Eevee will evolve a certain way with these names is because these were the names of the Eevee brothers in the Pokémon anime, and each had their own version of an evolved Eevee. There isn't necessarily a best version of which Pokémon you want Eevee to evolve into, although a lot of trainers seem to be a fan of Vaporeon. It's more a matter of whichever Pokémon you think is best. Just follow your instinct and pick which you want the most, and that Pokémon will be yours.

11. BATTLING AND DEFENDING GYMS

PICK A TEAM THAT YOU FEEL IS BEST

I switched Vaporeon to the front of the battle so he can get his strong attacks in early.

When you get to Level Five in the game, you have the chance to pick which team you want to be on, Team Valor, Team Mystic or Team Instinct. While there may be a bunch of kids at your school who are on Team Mystic, you should pick whichever team you feel is best. I was most intrigued by Team Valor, which is pretty interesting considering they're represented by the Pokémon Moltres while Team Instinct is represented by the Pokémon Zapdos, one of my favorites. Still, I followed my gut and picked Team Valor because they just seemed like the right team for me, and I haven't looked back since.

KNOW YOUR OPPONENTS' CP

This is quite possibly the most powerful Dragonite I've seen in the game.

This Electabuzz looks tough but its low CP suggests otherwise.

This Pidgeot is at a low CP so I could battle this gym and easily claim it for my team.

CP is a pretty good gauge of how strong a particular Pokémon will be in battle. If you have a water Pokémon with a high CP going against a fire Pokémon with a similar CP, you'll have a pretty good shot at winning. But if their CP is much higher than yours, you'll have to dodge a lot in battle. And if their CP is way higher than yours, it might be better to avoid the battle altogether until your Pokémon gets stronger. Don't be intimidated by CP; you can still win a lot of gym battles against Pokémon that are more powerful than you. Rather, CP should be used as a guide to help determine if that battle is even worth it from the get-go, whether it will be worth your time if you end up winning, or whether the loss will still mean something if you are defeated.

DON'T BE INTIMIDATED BY GYMS

This gym's Arcanine looks tough.

But the Pinsir makes me believe I have a shot at victory.

Just because there's a lot of high powered Pokémon at a certain gym doesn't mean that you should turn away. Defeating any number of those Pokémon will help reduce its prestige, and if it's an enemy gym, you'll still have six total Pokémon you can use in battle. Plus, any battle is a good opportunity to get practice at battling, so take the opportunity to fight stronger Pokémon. Who knows, you may end up winning.

BUT DON'T GO INTO POINTLESS BATTLES, EITHER

I had no strong Pokémon to fight against this Electabuzz, and now I'll have to use even more potions to heal them. This could have easily been avoided.

My Vaporeon might have been able to beat Arcanine if it had been at full health.

Something you will have to do after losing a battle or having your Pokémon defeated in battle is healing or reviving them. Healing requires potions, and reviving requires an item called Revive. You can only carry a certain amount of these at a time and if you go into too many overly-matched battles too often, you'll find yourself with a lack of items to heal your Pokémon. Then you won't be as strong to fight in Gym battles. Even if you want to conquer a gym in your team's name, you're not going to do yourself much good if your Pokémon are too weak to battle and you aren't able to heal them properly.

USE THE RIGHT TYPE OF POTIONS TO HEAL YOUR POKÉMON

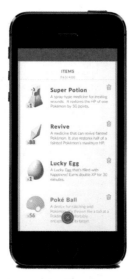 

A super potion is good to heal my stronger Pokémon, but might be more than necessary for my weaker.

All potions heal Pokémon injured in battle, but some heal better than others. Potions heal the smallest amount, while Super and Hyper potions heal more, and Max potions heal all. But Super, Hyper, and Max potions are harder to find, and you wouldn't want to use one of these more powerful potions on a Pokémon that could be healed perfectly by just a regular potion. Know which potions are best in which circumstances. It's better to use a hyper potion to heal a stronger Pokémon than lots of regular potions. You can still use regular potions to heal a more advanced Pokémon, although it'll take a lot more to get the job done. And you can use more advanced potions to heal a regular Pokémon fast when one or two regular potions would have done the job just fine. Just look to see what potion will work best for whatever situation you're in.

DON'T RUN OUT OF POTIONS OR REVIVES!

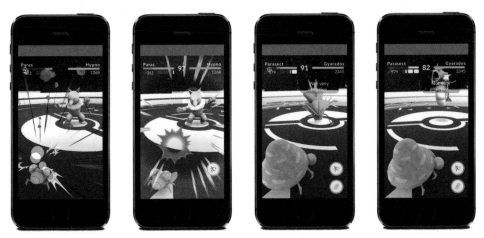

When I ran out of potions, I had to use weaker Pokémon in tough gym battles, and as you can see above, it didn't turn out too great.

Battling is a lot of fun, but you'll have to use a lot of potions to heal your Pokémon, and you may find yourself running out or completely empty. Then you'll be stuck having to collect more from PokéStops or leveling up before you can properly heal your Pokémon for them to battle again. Keep a good idea of how many potions and Revives you have on you, and if you notice yourself ever getting too low, take some time to collect some more before you head into battle again. You might even need to take a break from battling for a day or so just so you can actually get the necessary amount of potions and Revives to heal your Pokémon if they lose. But regardless of how often you battle, you will still need a steady supply of these items.

HELP RAISE YOUR TEAM'S PRESTIGE

Let's see if I can help raise prestige at this Team Valor gym.

I didn't defeat all of the Pokémon there, but those that I did beat still counted toward raising its prestige.

It's fun to claim gyms in your team's name, but it's equally as important to help raise the prestige of teams that are already managed by your team. If you're walking and see a gym that's being controlled by your team, train there and help raise its prestige to make sure it doesn't fall into a rival team's hands. Defeating any Pokémon on a gym's team will raise its prestige, so even if you only beat one or two and are defeated by the rest, you're still paying your team a good service. A good exercise would be to spend a few minutes every day going to gyms in your immediate area and help- ing raise prestige. Those five minutes at each gym can go a long way to helping it stay in your team's name that much longer. If you have a longer period of time throughout the day like thirty minutes or an hour to play the game, dedicate a certain portion of that time to raising team gym prestige wherever you may be.

PAY ATTENTION TO HOW MUCH PRESTIGE IS NEEDED TO DEFEAT A GYM

Each of these images gives a good idea of how much prestige is needed to get a gym under your control. Even if you lose a battle, look to see if you helped raise or reduce prestige at all, and what is still left for you to do.

There's a certain amount of prestige at each gym that needs to be reduced before it can be claimed for another team. If you visit an enemy gym and see it has a prestige of ten thousand and you only have a small amount of potions and not as strong Pokémon, it may not be worth fighting. But if a gym is at a prestige of fifteen hundred, you won't have to do much to reduce it to zero and claim it for your team. All of this is a matter of whether or not that gym is one worth claiming for your team, whether you have a Pokémon you want to defend it, or whether or not you can spend a lot of time raising the prestige of your own team's gym. Knowing how much prestige is necessary to topple or strengthen a gym will help you determine how much time you need to accomplish your goal, and if it is even worth it at all.

PICK A WELL-BALANCED "TYPE" TEAM

Vaporeon, Onix, and Rhydon all pack a punch. But I could
have replaced Onix or Rhydon with another Pokémon
that wasn't a ground type to give it more diversity.

If you're going against a gym that has a diverse group
of Pokémon with different types, you'll want to make
sure that your group of Pokémon is also diverse, both in
type, power of attacks, and CP level. Choose Pokémon
with a variety of types that have specific strengths over
those Pokémon at that gym, and you'll be in good posi-
tion to win the battle.

Here's a good reminder of which Pokémon types are
stronger against others. Lots of Pokémon can have more
than one type, and sometimes type doesn't even matter
at all if a certain Pokémon is strong enough. But type is a
handy way to pick out your Pokémon for battle, to know
what your respective strengths and weaknesses are, and
then be able to capitalize on that for battle victory.

Fire Pokémon are stronger against Grass, Ice, and Bug types. They are weaker against Water, Ground, and Rock types.

Water Pokémon are stronger against Fire, Ground, and Rock types. They're weaker against Grass and Dragon types.

Electric Pokémon are stronger against Water and Flying types. They're weaker against Grass, Ground, and Dragon types.

Grass Pokémon are stronger against Water, Ground, and Rock types. They're weaker against Fire, Poison, Flying, Bug, and Dragon types.

Ice Pokémon are stronger against Grass, Ground, Flying, and Dragon types. They're weaker against Water types.

Fighting Pokémon are stronger against Normal, Ice, and Rock types. They're weaker against Poison, Psychic, Flying, Bug, or Ghost types.

Poison Pokémon are stronger against Grass and Bug types. They're weaker against Ground, Rock, and Ghost types.

Ground Pokémon are stronger against Fire, Electric, Poison, and Rock types. They're weaker against Grass, Flying, and Bug types.

Flying Pokémon are stronger against Grass, Fighting, and Bug types. They're weaker against Electric and Rock types.

Psychic Pokémon are stronger against Fighting and Poison types.

Bug Pokémon are stronger against Grass, Poison, and Psychic types. They're weaker against Fire, Fighting, and Psychic types.

Rock Pokémon are stronger against Fire, Ice, Ground, and Bug types. They're weaker against Fighting and Ground types.

KNOW WHICH OF YOUR POKÉMON HAVE THE STRONGEST ATTACKS

Vaporeon has a decent special attack, although its regular attack isn't anything incredible.

Raichu balances good regular attack damage with specific attack damage.

If you've ever wondered why Arcanine is so popular, look at its damage for Fire, one of its special attacks.

If you look at the Pokémon and select a monster, you'll be able to see a number next to each of that monster's attacks. This indicates how much damage that attack will cause an opponent, and gives a good idea of which will be better in battle. It's good to have a well-balanced team of different types, but you'll also want to select Pokémon who can lay down the punches as well. If you're going against a high CP Pokémon, you can guess that monster will have a pretty high HP to go along with it, and whatever Pokémon you choose will need the most powerful attacks to help bring it down. But if you're going against a Pokémon whose CP is around the same as yours or lower, you can still hold your own in battle, even if your attacks aren't exactly earth-shaking.

BECOME A MASTER AT DODGING

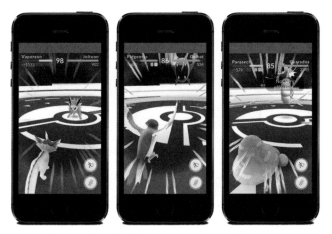

That yellow flash means you need to move quick to dodge.

And if you pull it off right, you should be able to not suffer as much damage, if any.

Dodging, arguably, is the most important skill you can learn in battle as it'll be the thing that helps keep your Pokémon's damage low, and helps keep you alive long enough to dish out attacks to defeat your opponent. Pay attention to the yellow flash that appears on screen during an attack. Time it correctly, and dodge. Continue dodging throughout the fight, don't just dodge one special attack and think things are over. Dodging won't win you every battle, and there'll be a lot of times when you think you've timed your dodge perfectly, but you still get attacked by your opponent. Participate in enough battles to learn this skill perfectly, as it will often be the deal breaker between a victory or defeat.

BUT KNOW WHEN TO ATTACK AS WELL

Don't just stand in the corner, give those Pokémon everything you've got!

Even if you dodge every enemy attack, you'll still need to attack them enough to reduce their Hit Points or HP to zero to defeat that Pokémon. The battle isn't won just by the Pokémon with the highest amount of HP, you actually need to reduce the other Pokémon's HP to zero to win. Attack quickly, and know how to attack when it's the right moment in between your opponent's attacks and when you're not busy dodging. If your Pokémon is at a high enough CP compared to your opponent's, it might be worth it just to take their damage and spend a lot of time attacking. You might have little HP left at the end of the battle, but a win is still a win, regardless of how damaged your Pokémon may be.

KNOW WHICH POKÉMON TO LEAVE AT A GYM

This Omastar was a great choice to leave at the gym, since there aren't many Water Pokémon in this area.

This Jolteon has a pretty low CP compared to similar Pokémon, and may not have been the best choice to leave behind.

It may seem like a good idea to leave your strongest Pokémon at a gym that you conquered, since they're going to be the ones most likely to defend it longer, right? Not always, because if you want to conquer more gyms, you'll want that stronger Pokémon in your possession. But you also don't want to leave a weaker Pokémon guarding a gym either, since they can be easily defeated and you won't get as many PokéCoins . Ask yourself which Pokémon you don't mind giving up to guard that gym, and which are strong enough to hold that gym over for a while. You probably won't have a Pokémon at that gym forever—another team will come along and defeat it, but you'll still want one there as long as you can.

ALSO, PICK A POKÉMON TO DEFEND A GYM THAT HAS A STRENGTH OVER OTHER TYPES IN THAT AREA

Growlithe may hold an elemental advantage over grass types, but I'ts not really that powerful

Hypno though has few weaknesses being a psychic type, and is always a tough opponent in battle.

A lot of Grass- and Rock-type Pokémon appear where I live, and at the gyms in my neighborhood, I see a lot of Pokémon of those types defending them. Whenever you do have a Pokémon defending a gym, pick one who is stronger than the other Pokémon that would appear in that area. For example, it might be better to use an Electric Pokémon to defend a gym if a lot of Water Pokémon appear near there. This way if nearby trainers with those Water Pokémon battle at my gym, I'll hold an advantage. This doesn't mean that every trainer has the same Pokémon in any given location, but you make a good guess as to which would hold a gym better based on what Pokémon you see appear near there.

PAY ATTENTION TO THE CLOCK

I have lots of time in each of these scenarios, except for Tentacruel where I have just eighty seconds. Still, that clock can move quickly so watch out.

You still only have a certain amount of time to win gym battles, and it's easy to lose track of that if you're busy dodging or just attacking in small portions. Before you know it, if you're not paying attention to the clock, you might receive a message that time is up, and you'll end up losing your gym battle. The clock is going to run out regardless sometimes, and there will be many battles where it feels like you don't have the time you need to win. Pay attention to the clock and know just how much time you have left, and use that amount of time to determine just how much you'll need to attack and which to dodge.

DON'T RELY ON A FAVORITE

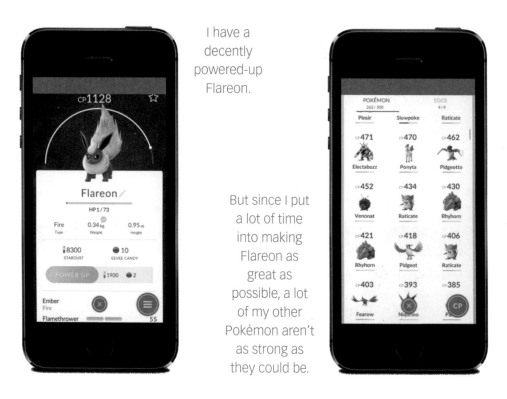

I have a decently powered-up Flareon.

But since I put a lot of time into making Flareon as great as possible, a lot of my other Pokémon aren't as strong as they could be.

It's easy to get into the habit of just powering up one of your favorite Pokémon over and over, and not taking the time to invest in your other monsters. When you do power up Pokémon, make sure to power up multiple at a time and have a good balance of strong monsters in your collection. Otherwise, your team will be unbalanced in battle and you won't be able to claim gyms as easily. If you power up your Electabuzz over and over again, it'll be a very powerful Pokémon to contend with but will leave you with a lot of monsters that are underdeveloped in the rest of your collection. Then you'll have difficulty winning and doing well in battles. There's nothing wrong with having a favorite Pokémon, but only making your favorite powerful is a bad idea.

TRY AT THE SAME GYM MULTIPLE TIMES

I've become very acquainted with this gym being defended by Omastar.

These gyms may be tough, but if my Pokémon are in good shape and I have a good amount of potions, no reason why I can't try again.

Just because you got defeated once at a gym doesn't mean you should walk away. Only by practicing more and more at that gym will you be able to learn how those specific Pokémon attack, and how to best approach them in battle. Sometimes you'll need to fight them five times to defeat all of them, sometimes it'll be ten or more, but only with practice will you be able to figure out how to defeat those Pokémon. Only do this if you have enough potions and Revives to keep your Pokémon up to speed. But battling a few times will help you learn those other Pokémon's attacks. I had to battle at this gym multiple times to finally defeat this powerful Arcanine, but eventually I became familiar enough with its attack pattern and knowing when to dodge that I was able to trounce over it.

KNOW WHEN TO SWAP POKÉMON IN BATTLE

This Paras isn't going to do much against Gyrados, another Water type.

Nor is my weak Onix against Tentacruel.

In the heat of battle, it's easy to forget that you can swap out your Pokémon for others who might fare better against a certain opponent. You can organize the order of what monster you want to appear before a battle even starts, but in the middle of fighting, you might discover that one of your Pokémon's quicker attacks would be better against a slower Pokémon. Or if there's a certain elemental weakness you didn't take into account before battling, swapping Pokémon out will help you overcome that. While my Vaporeon is easily my favorite Pokémon to use in battle, it isn't necessarily great to use against other Water types or a Grass or Electric type. In those situations, I'll swap out Vaporeon for another strong Pokémon in my collection, or perhaps a Pokémon who holds a strong elemental strength over another opponent.

12. BATTLE CHALLENGES

DEFEAT A GYM CONTROLLED BY YOUR OWN TEAM

Team Mystic members would love to battle at this gym, since the yellow Electabuzz is defending it.

If I was team Mystic, this would be a great gym to train at.

This gives a good idea of what your particular Pokémon's strengths and weaknesses are in battle, as well as helping you become accustomed to dodging and moving. Completing this challenge will show you have some early talent to be a true battle master. It'll also give you an idea of how easily your gym can fall into opponent's hands. If you defeat the gym monsters pretty easily, it'll still help raise that gym's prestige, but also show how easily those Pokémon are defeated. This is why you should help raise prestige at any gyms you can, even just battling a few Pokémon for a few minutes and winning will go a long way to help keep that gym in your team's name.

DEFEAT AN ENEMY GYM USING ONLY ONE POKÉMON

This Gyrados is powered-up enough it could defeat six Pokémon in battle if it wanted to on its own, and then some.

It'll be very difficult to defeat this Snorlax with one Pokémon, but I can still try.

You get to pick six, but try to defeat all of the opposing Pokémon in a gym using only one of your own Pokémon. It'll be very difficult as it could be five or more Pokémon vs. one, and you'll probably have less and less HP in each battle. But this will teach you how to best control your attacks, dodging, and use of time in battle. To make this challenge more interesting, try defeating the gym without taking any damage at all. You'll need to do a lot of dodging, but it may be possible to pull off. You can also try not moving at all and see if you can defeat your opponent just by sitting in one spot and attacking over and over again. While this isn't as challenging, it is certainly fun and gives you an idea of how powerful your Pokémon may be compared to other Pokémon.

DEFEAT AN ENEMY GYM WITH FIVE THOUSAND PRESTIGE

This Team Instinct gym is a good place to start before battling at that Team Mystic gym down the road.

Some gyms are pretty easy to defeat, with a few weaker Pokémon being the only thing between you and success. But gyms with five thousand prestige or more are pretty difficult, with a lot of different Pokémon ready to show you what they've got. This challenge will prove how far you've come in your battling skills, and give you a good idea of how much more difficult gyms can become in the game. It'll also show that while some gyms may seem very difficult to defeat at first, all you need to do is become better at battling and powering up your Pokémon and there's no reason why you can't defeat any gym.

DEFEAT A LEVEL TEN GYM

This Snorlax is not messing around at this Level Ten gym.

This gym was very hard to defeat.

It may seem impossible, it may be incredibly difficult, but his challenge will show whether or not you're ready to be one of the best, and what you need to do to power up your Pokémon and get them ready for the best. Then when you're successful and you may claim the gym in your team's name, you'll be able to show off your true battle skills to all the trainers around you. What's funny about gyms though is that you often don't remember the name of the trainer who is controlling them. You see an intimidating Pokémon like Gyrados or Snorlax, but rarely pay attention to the trainers who made those Pokémon so powerful in the first place. This will help you remember those trainers and the powerful players in your area, and help you stay at their level. That way when you see another powerful Pokémon in your area, you'll be able to tell if it was controlled by one of the powerful trainers you defeated.

REDUCE AN ENEMY GYM'S PRESTIGE TO ZERO IN LESS THAN AN HOUR

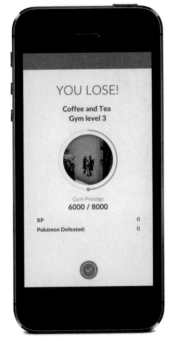

I'll have to beat Exeggutor many times if I want to complete this challenge.

Only 6,000 prestige left to go? You could do that in an hour with the right items and powered-up Pokémon.

There isn't necessarily a set level of prestige for this challenge, but this is more to teach you how to battle quickly and how to effectively claim gyms in your team's name. Take some pictures while you're at it. It'll also give you a good idea of what goes into defeating an enemy gym, and how quickly a gym that's controlled in your team's name can fall to zero really quickly. If you know a lot of people who also play Pokémon GO and are on the same team as you, have them participate in this challenge as well. This way you'll be able to build up a very strong gym on your own, and as a group, will be easily able to topple enemy gyms as fast as possible.

DEFEND A GYM FOR A FULL DAY

This Venonat is cute but will probably get defeated early on, and wouldn't be able to hold a gym for a day.

This Flareon probably couldn't hold its own if it was defending a gym all day by itself.

So you've won your battle and claimed a gym. Now what? It's time to defend it! See if you can defend a gym for a full day with a Pokémon. You'll know if you didn't if that Pokémon appears back in your collection without the little marker noting it was at a gym. If you can make it a full day, you'll know you're well on your way to being a master. And if not, it'll show you still need to power up your Pokémon more. A good idea would be to look at other gyms in the nearby area to see which types of Pokémon they have defending them, and then choose something a bit different.

DEFEND TEN GYMS AT THE SAME TIME

These Pokémon are pretty strong for battle, but I also need to choose which I would want to leave behind to defend a gym.

You'll need to put in a lot of footwork for this one.

This is really difficult, as you'll not only have had to conquer ten gyms, but also have Pokémon strong enough to hold them over as you go on to claim each new one. Having your Pokémon at high CP levels and being able to go to a lot of different gyms in a short amount of time will help you succeed at this challenge. This will prove that you are a great battler and gym defender, and that you are wise about which Pokémon to evolve and power up.

GO THROUGH THE ENTIRE GAME WITHOUT PURCHASING EXTRA POKÉCOINS IN THE SHOP

Five hundred ninety PokéCoins can go a long way.

You can still accomplish everything you need to in the game just by collecting XP.

This is a difficult one, since aside from the shop, Poké-Coins are only gained from gyms. And depending how fast your Pokémon are defeated, you may not earn coins that quickly. This will show you the time that goes into collecting coins, and how you have to be careful about what items you buy in the shop since you only have a certain amount. You'll have to defend a lot of different gyms for a long time to accomplish this, but it'll show you just how valuable PokéCoins are, while also helping you get that much better at battling and powering up your Pokémon.

13. HATCHING EGGS

WALK IN A STRAIGHT LINE

This street stays straight for miles, and is a good place to hatch eggs by walking.

Since the game determines how far you've walked by checking in on where you were at one moment and where you were at another, it's most beneficial to walk in a straight line to make sure you're not losing out on any footwork while hatching eggs. Taking lots of turns while walking make the game not count your egg hatching correctly. If there's an egg you really want to hatch, find an area where you know you could walk that distance and that you can stay on a straight line as much as possible. Moving around a bit here and there won't cause that much damage, but the sooner you walk in a straight line, the better.

DRIVING AND CHEATING AREN'T BETTER

You're going to have to walk those streets if you want to catch those eggs.

To hatch eggs, you'll need to walk. A lot.

Driving is a good way to explore new areas but not to hatch new eggs. Walking is the best way, and driving distances won't count. There are other ways players have tried to hatch their eggs more quickly, some have attached their phones to their dogs and played fetch, getting those distance points as their dogs ran around. Others have even attached their phones to a turntable, and it spun around just slowly enough that it counted for distance. But really, putting in a lot of time and effort into finding a strange way to hatch an egg takes more effort than actually walking that specific distance to hatch it.

SWAP OUT EGGS AS SOON AS THEY HATCH

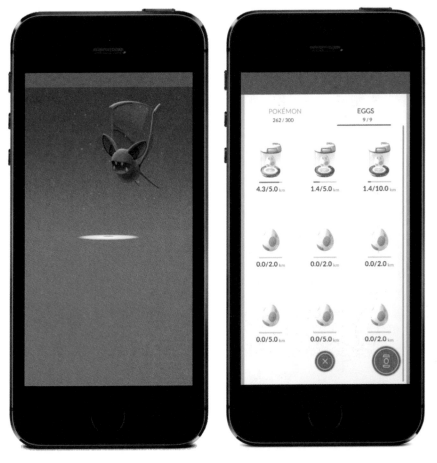

Right after the top left egg hatches, I'll want to start incubating another one right away.

Once you're done hatching an egg, start hatching another one! This requires you to have a steady supply of incubators, and also a lot of time to continue walking to hatch that new egg. While immediately incubating a new egg doesn't make it hatch any faster, it is believed that hatching it as soon as possible will lead to rarer Pokémon. No reason to lose all that distance you walked; you want to make sure every step counts.

KNOW WHICH EGGS TO HATCH FIRST

They all appear the same, but I should go for that ten km egg in the bottom row.

For the most part, but not always, eggs with a higher distance requirement hatch rarer monsters. These are the ones you want to start hatching first, rather than the two km eggs. This also requires the most amount of walking, as ten km is much more than five or two km. But in the name of getting rare Pokémon, it may just be worth it. Even if you only find yourself with a bunch of two km eggs, they're still worth hatching as you're out walking and playing the game anyway. And you'll get additional XP, too.

DON'T GET DISAPPOINTED IF YOU DON'T GET A POKÉMON YOU WANT

Hatching a Nidoran was disappointing but I just had to move on and find a new egg to hatch.

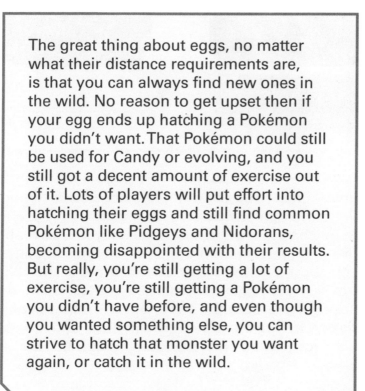

The great thing about eggs, no matter what their distance requirements are, is that you can always find new ones in the wild. No reason to get upset then if your egg ends up hatching a Pokémon you didn't want. That Pokémon could still be used for Candy or evolving, and you still got a decent amount of exercise out of it. Lots of players will put effort into hatching their eggs and still find common Pokémon like Pidgeys and Nidorans, becoming disappointed with their results. But really, you're still getting a lot of exercise, you're still getting a Pokémon you didn't have before, and even though you wanted something else, you can strive to hatch that monster you want again, or catch it in the wild.

KEEP A GOOD STOCK OF INCUBATORS

You're going to want more than just the one infinite incubator.

Two or three is a good amount to start with.

You have only one incubator that can be used an infinite amount of times, and the others expire after a certain amount of uses. Make sure you have plenty of incubators to hatch as many eggs as you need. There's really no reason, if you have more than three eggs at one time, that you shouldn't be trying to hatch three of those. This requires actively playing the game to obtain them, or purchasing them from the shop. But ask for an adult's permission before buying any incubators, and if they say no, you'll just have to play the game that much harder to get more.

KEEP TRACK OF HOW MUCH TIME YOU NEED TO HATCH AN EGG

There's more than enough roads for me to walk down to hatch an egg here.

0/10 km

Use an incubator to incubate this Egg.

START INCUBATION

If I plan this correctly, I could go on a ten km bike ride, or ten one km jogs throughout the week to hatch this egg.

Knowing you have to walk ten km, or just about six miles, to hatch an egg seems like a lot of work. Each egg has a metric distance requirement listed under it— ten, five, or two km. By looking under each egg, you'll know ahead of time and can plan where you need to walk to hatch it. Sometimes I'll see I have five km needed to hatch a ten km egg, and I'll focus my afternoon workout around getting that egg hatched. Some players also keep a specific foot timer, either with their phone, watch or other device, so they know exactly how far they've traveled and how much more they need to go.

DON'T USE THE WRONG INCUBATOR

Should probably use the infinite
and save the others for later.

If you have only one egg in your possession, it's better to use the infinite incubator rather than an incubator that only has a limited amount of uses. This will help you keep the amount of incubators you have clean, instead of having a bunch that can only be used one or to two times. You can't really ever misuse an incubator—your infinite incubator is still always going to be infinite, and your other incubators are going to run out of uses, regardless of what order you use them in. This tip is more about keeping them all organized instead of having a dozen incubators with only one turn left.

14. THE SINGLE MOST IMPORTANT THINGS TO REMEMBER IN POKÉMON GO

FIND FUN LOCATIONS TO TAKE LOTS OF PICTURES

Getting ready to take a picture of Rattata.

Pikachu hanging out on the bushes.

Clefairy at a
concert.

Eevee helping me with
my sandwich order.

Venonat getting my
guacamole dirty.

It doesn't matter if you're playing Pokémon GO somewhere like at a baseball game or a concert, or you're just relaxing and playing with your family at home, taking pictures of your Pokémon is one of the most fun parts of being a trainer. Take as many as you want by pressing the camera button when catching. A lot of smartphones also allow you to take a screenshot, so you can try that too.

These pictures can either be in battle or in the middle of catching Pokémon, but find five different locations where you can take pictures that are funny, creative, and unique. Some place where pictures are allowed but at the same time, places where you wouldn't normally think to take a picture. I captured some really funny images while I was waiting in line to order some food, or even when I was sitting in the stands at a baseball game. Try to think creatively too, if you take a picture of something further away that'll make your Pokémon a lot bigger. And if you take a picture of something up close, that'll make your Pokémon look a lot smaller. Be creative and don't be afraid to share some of your best photos with friends. Just be conscious though of where you are taking pictures. Sometimes a camera might not be allowed there, and other times it might be rude or inappropriate to take other people's pictures.

DON'T GET DISTRACTED WHILE PLAYING THE GAME

The game isn't joking when it says this.

I wanted the information behind this sign, but was so into the game that I bumped into someone walking down the sidewalk.

You don't want to be walking around somewhere, playing Pokémon GO, and accidentally walk into something or trip and fall because you weren't paying attention. Always be aware of your surroundings, and take a break from the game and look up every few seconds, just so you always have a good idea of where you are and where you are going in real life. Even if you're riding in a car or playing the game while walking with your family somewhere, it's very easy to become distracted by everything that's going on and lose track of where you are.

DO EVERYTHING YOU CAN TO GET XP

Fighting in battles is just one of the many ways you can get XP.

Catch easy Pokémon even if you don't want them (although you should never say no to Caterpie.)

Leveling up makes Pokémon GO a more fun experience, and the only way to level up is by gaining XP. Catching Pokémon, evolving them, visiting PokéStops, training and battling at gyms, and hatching eggs are all things that help you gain XP and help make you that much better a trainer. While getting more XP will help you level up more quickly, it shouldn't be your primary focus. You want to battle primarily to win battles, and you want to catch Pokémon for the sake of catching Pokémon. XP is a useful and important thing but it isn't the main thing you should be trying to accomplish in the game. Do as much as possible in the game and have fun doing so, and from that, you'll see the XP start to pour in.

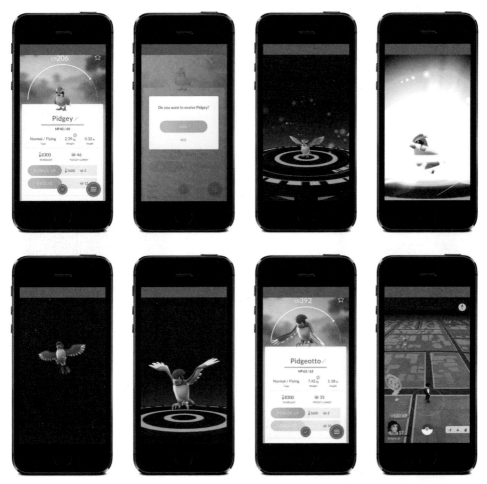

I didn't care about this Pidgey or even want a Pidgeotto, but I got five hundred
XP from evolving it, making it that much more worthwhile.

Gaining a lot of XP can be difficult, especially if there
are few PokéStops for you to visit, few Pokémon to
catch, or if you're really just not ready to fight at certain
gyms. Using a lucky egg can make gaining XP a faster
process, as you'll earn double the amount for anything
you do that would give XP in a thirty minute window.

This item is going to be your best
friend when gaining XP.

Lucky eggs, though, like any item, aren't infinite; you
have to earn them in the game or buy them in the shop,
and you don't necessarily want to use a lucky egg if you
don't have that full thirty minutes to get the full effects
from them. Make sure you actually do have that time
and that there is nothing to distract you from playing
the game, and that way you'll truly maximize on the
possible amount of XP you can earn.

AND THE SINGLE MOST IMPORTANT TIP OF ALL FOR PLAYING POKÉMON GO . . .

It isn't about catching the most . . .

It isn't about getting as many items as possible . . .

Or defeating as many opponents in battles as you can . . .

The most important thing that you need to remember, above all else while you're playing Pokémon GO: **HAVE FUN.** There will be some times when you get disappointed because you didn't catch a Pokémon you wanted, or because you lost a battle that you were trying really hard to win. Just remember that Pokémon GO is all about exploring and doing new things, and there's always room for second chances.

The best Pokémon GO players are the ones who don't take it too seriously, those who still get excited when they win at a gym battle or catch a rare Pokémon, but at the same time don't let it ruin their day if that doesn't happen. Above all else, make sure you're having fun while you're playing Pokémon GO. Explore lots of new areas, see a lot of cool monsters you didn't see before, take some funny pictures and test your strength in gym battles, not so you can be better than everyone else at the game, but so you can have the most amount of fun. Above all else, making fun your main priority will make you a true Pokémon GO master.

Go capture some fun!